This book belongs to:

_____

When I was little, all I dreamed about was being grown-up. I couldn't wait for the freedom and adventures. But little did I know, being grown isn't always easy. Even so, I wouldn't trade my life for anything—because now, I have you, my little ones, and my handsome husband who I love so much! the love of a family means the world to me.
Thank you, God

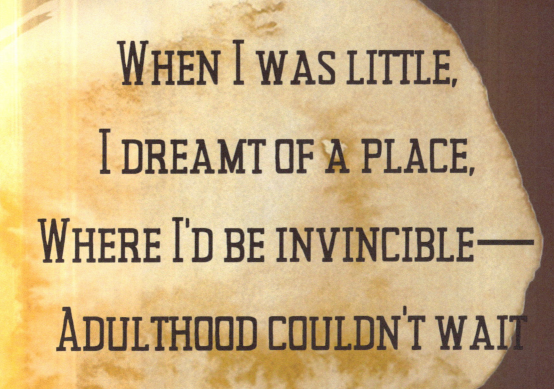

When I was little,
I dreamt of a place,
Where I'd be invincible—
Adulthood couldn't wait

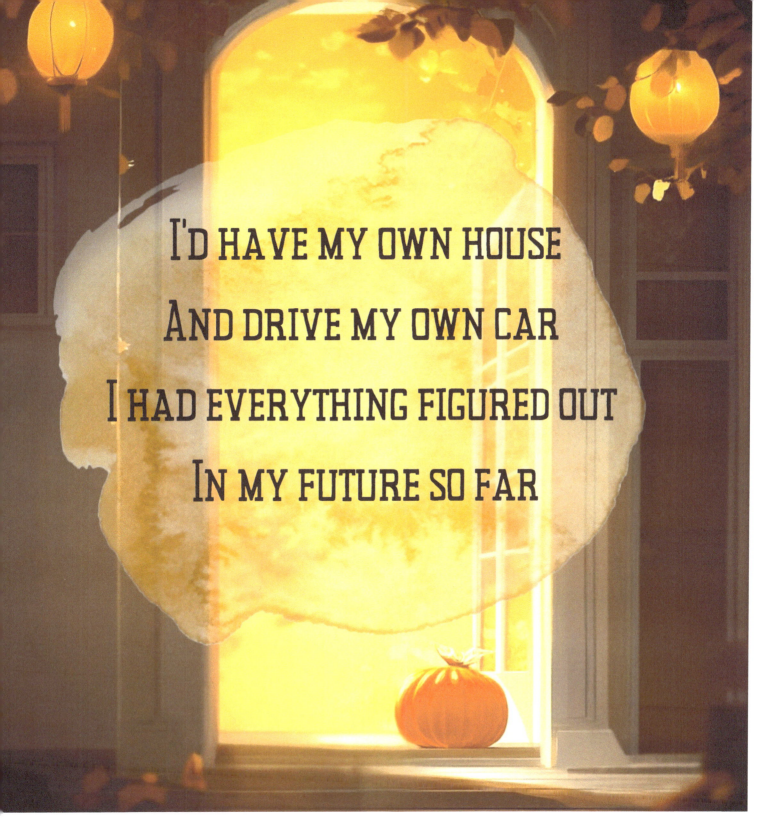

I pictured my husband,
The wait would be worth it
A fairytale ending,
Everything perfect

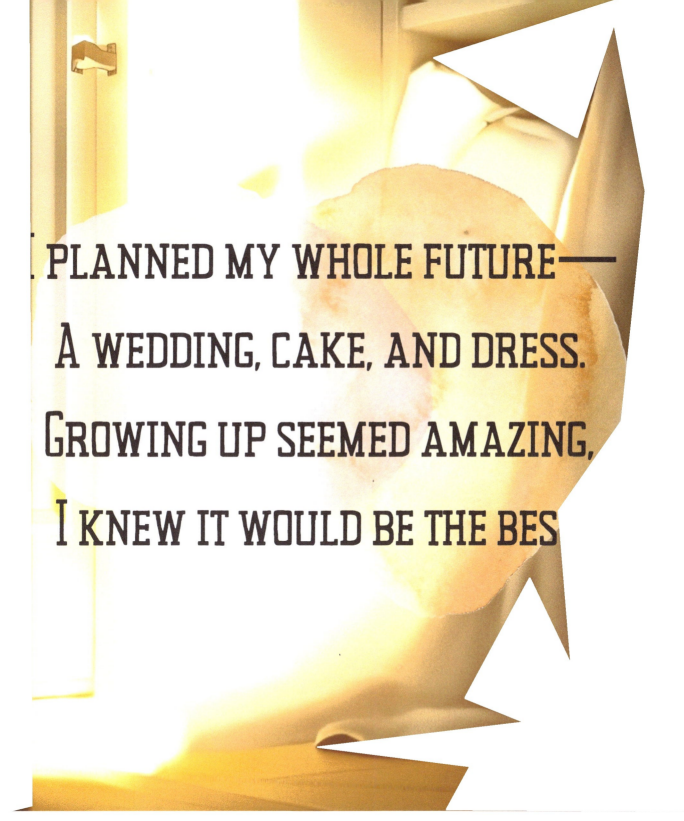

I planned my whole future—
A wedding, cake, and dress.
Growing up seemed amazing,
I knew it would be the bes

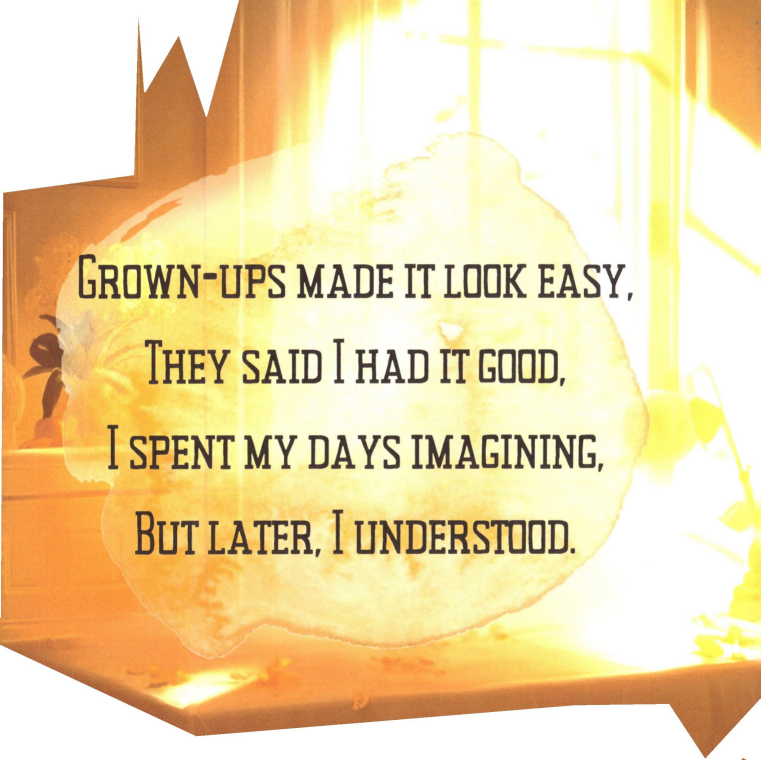

Little me, just wait...
You don't need to rush and grow up
There's no napping here for days...
Just baby poop and throw up

You'll cook and you'll clean
With little time for anything else
Care for your toddlers and dream
Of when you were once little yourself

"Dear little me,"
I can't use the bathroom alone!
I have kids at my feet,
Always waiting for Mom.

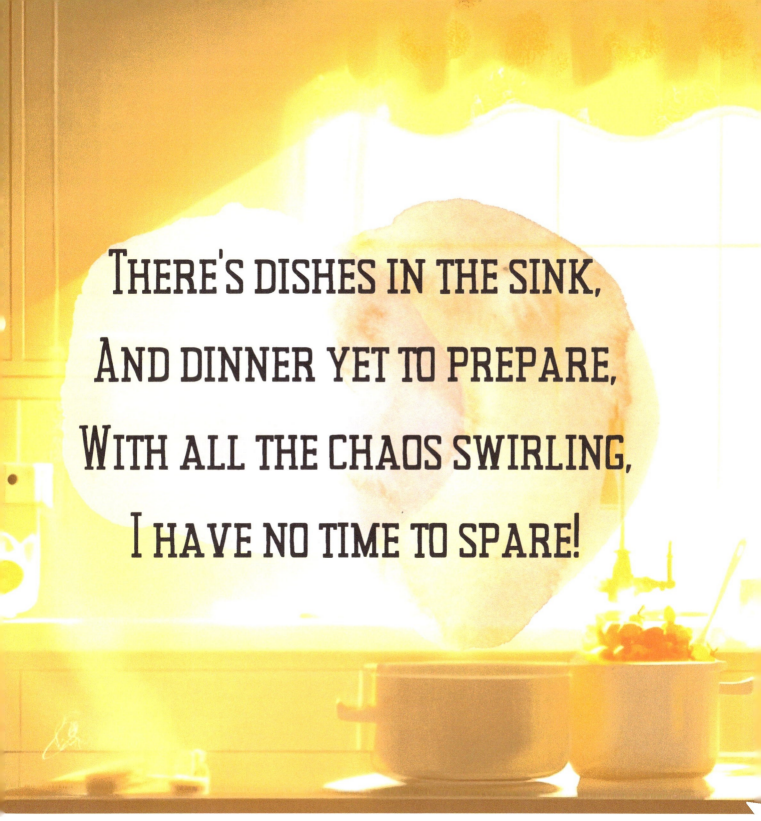

If for a day, I could trade

Or in time, just go back

To where my bills were all paid

And I was forced to take a nap

"Book me a ticket,"

I'd head right to the station.

What a treat it would be,

A mini vacation!

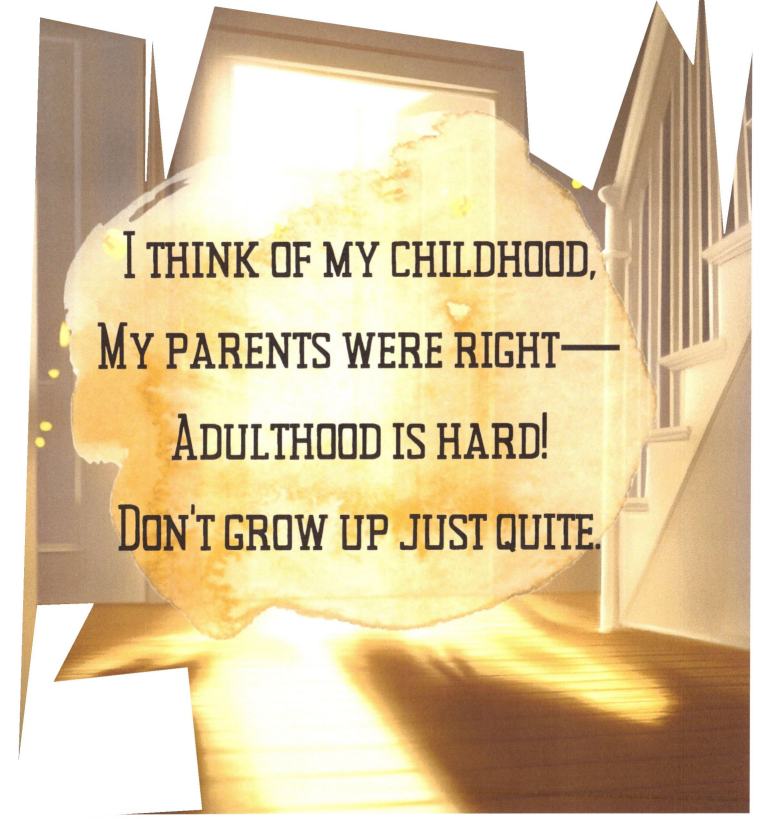

As I hide in this closet

I'm sitting in the very back

Under a big blanket

With a yummy chocolate snack

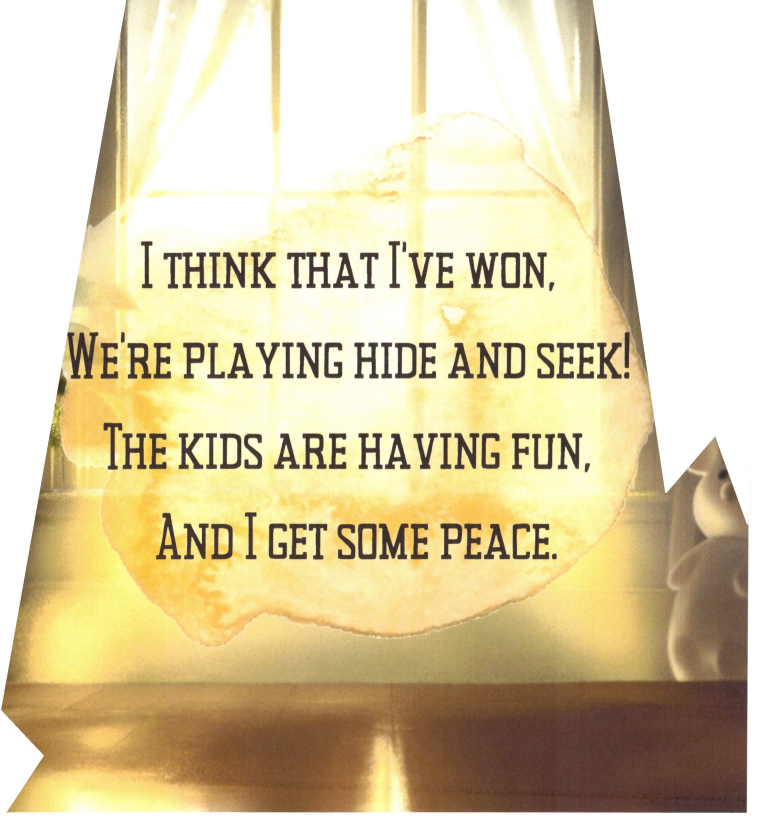

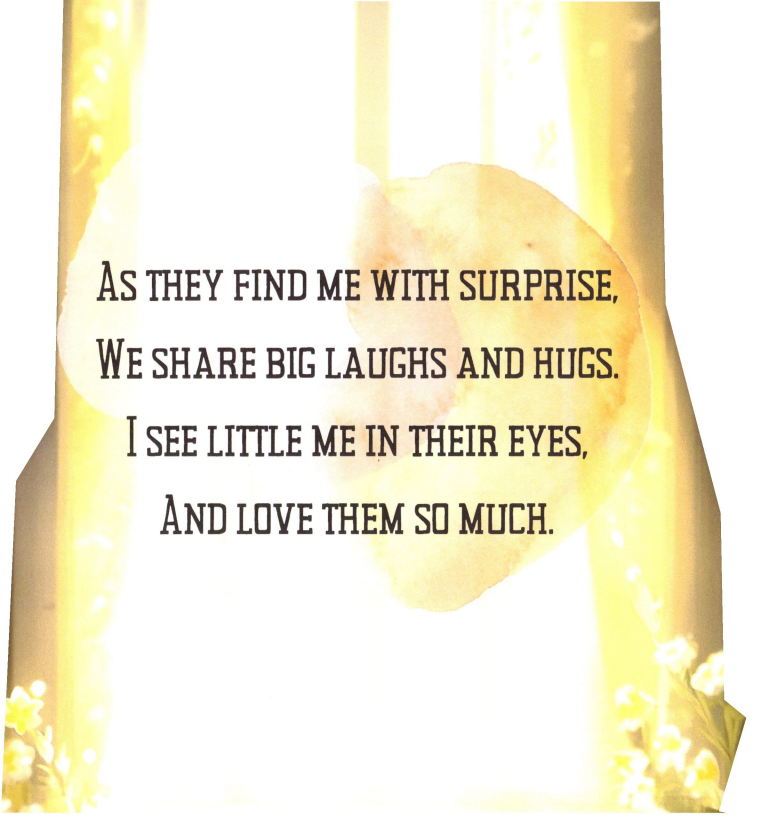

As they find me with surprise,
We share big laughs and hugs.
I see little me in their eyes,
And love them so much.

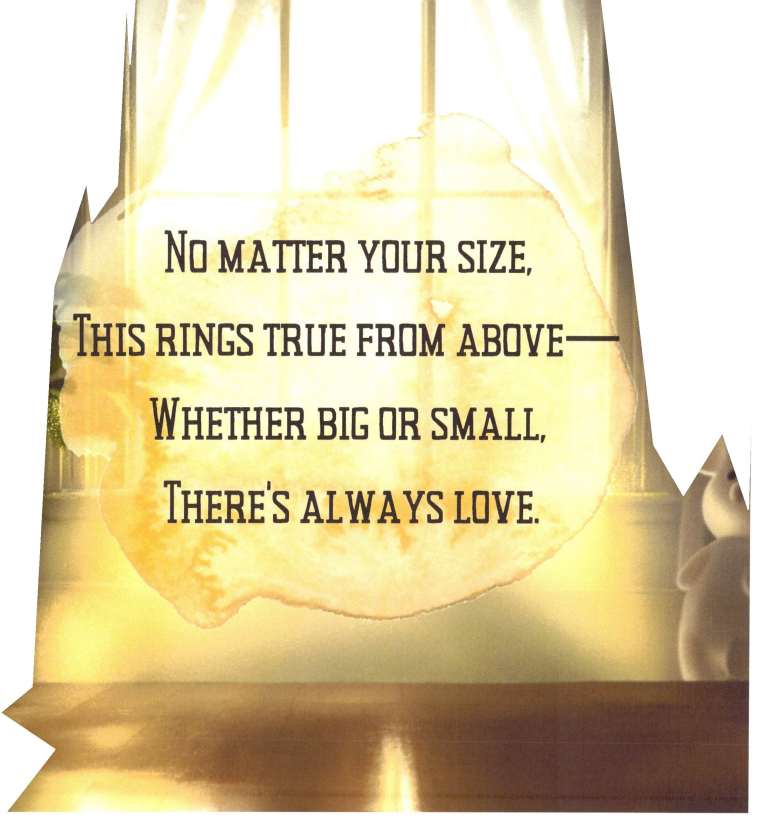

No matter your size,
This rings true from above—
Whether big or small,
There's always love.

Milton Keynes UK
Ingram Content Group UK Ltd.
UKHW051158251124
451531UK00002B/6